Minute Taking Madness

How to write clear, concise and condensed minutes and still keep your sanity!

By Robyn Bennett

Cover design by Lynn O'Shea
Freshfields Graphic Design
Info@ffieldsdesign.co.nz

ISBN: (softcover) 978-0-473-37587-4
ISBN: (Epub) 978-0-473-37588-1
ISBN: (Kindle) 978-0-37763-2
ISBN: (PDF) 978-0-37589-8
ISBN: (ibook) 978-0-473-37590-4

Table of Contents

Robyn Bennett

Over the past ten years, Robyn has led in excess of 500 plus minute taking courses for over 1,000 participants. She runs the popular The Art of Minute Taking course at Victoria University of Wellington, New Zealand where it was the top Professional and Executive Development course for 2015 and 2016.

Robyn has developed systems and processes round the best way to write minutes and is passionate about sharing these with others who strive to be excellent minute takers.

Robyn has previously worked as an Executive Assistant and a contract minute taker. She is a past National President of the Association of Administrative Professionals New Zealand Inc.

Testimonials

This is awesome! I can't say enough about how Minute Taking Madness is tailored to the needs of the minute taker. Robyn, you were my inspiration behind becoming a better minute taker! Your minute taking courses got me up and running and this book will be a good reference tool for me. Highly recommend this to any minute taker.

Tendai Nyamdela, Founder - ExcelleNZ AssistaNZ, New Zealand

Robyn has created a book overflowing with secrets, tips and tools of the trade in a practical and humorous read. Whether you have been taking minutes for twenty minutes or twenty years, this book has something for you. You will find yourself referring to it again and again and you might even find yourself enjoying taking minutes!

Sherie Pointon – Admin Advantage, New Zealand

Dedication

To all the world's minute takers

Be proud of what you do

Minute taking – A beast of burden?

Congratulations – you're reading this because you've been taking minutes for a while and are looking for something to verify that what you're doing is right.

Or you're facing a fear – if you work in administration it's very much an occupational hazard that during one stage in your career you'll be taking minutes. And the fear arises from the fact that most people have never had any training in minute taking so they're never sure if what they're doing is right.

This book will help you to demystify some of the questions round minute taking and write minutes like the true professional you are!

The book has been structured with a summary at the end of each chapter and some exercises or an action plan to help you put into practise the main points covered.

Chapter 1 – Common challenges for minute takers

As a minute taker trainer one of the questions I always ask at the beginning of my courses is, "Who likes taking minutes?" Generally, nobody puts their hand up. A few people say, "I don't mind it." Most people vigorously shake their heads. They avoid minute taking like the plague!

This is backed up by a survey undertaken by Office Team a number of years ago. They surveyed 1,050 administrators round the world and asked them two questions: What did they like best in their job? and What did they like least in their job? Not surprisingly for the second question it was minute taking that came out at the top (32 percent).

The next question I ask is; "What are your common challenges in minute taking? What is it about minute taking you don't like?"

And here are the common challenges with suggested solutions:

How much detail should I put in my minutes

Solution: See Chapters 10 and 11.

Meetings that digress from the agenda

Solution: Fire the chairman! No, seriously. See Chapter 4.

Meeting behaviour

Solution: See Chapter 4.

I'm writing a book!

Solution: See Chapter 10 – Common challenges for minute takers and Chapters 11 and 12 – Determining what needs to be recorded.

Understanding the subject, acronyms and jargon

This is a biggie! We talk and write so much these days in abbreviated form and acronyms are everywhere.

One meeting I had to take minutes at involved the acronym – HSNO – something I'd never heard before. It stands for Hazardous Substances and New Organisms. The way you say it is, "has no". In this meeting someone started talking and then in the middle said this "has no". I was thinking, "Has no what?" Other people in the meeting were also using the phrase "has no". This went on for about 10 minutes and I was becoming extremely frustrated wondering what people were talking about. But it appeared I wasn't the only one who was getting confused. Eventually someone pointed out that "has no" was the Hazardous Substances and New Organisms. I could hear people going, "Ahh!" It was now making sense.

Solution: Preparation is the key.

- Prepare yourself thoroughly before the meeting by reading the agenda and background papers.

- Ask people to explain anything if you don't understand the terminology or subject matter.

- If it's a meeting that has an established history and it's your first time, read at least the last three sets of minutes. Doing this will help you pick up the story behind the issues and will forewarn you of acronyms and jargon that may arise.

- Does your organisation have a glossary? A quick look at this might help you get familiar with some of the terms. Remember to use the Internet - Google is your best friend!

Knowledge is something you'll gain as you become more familiar with the subject. So keep going to the meetings (please don't hate me for saying that!).

People who talk too fast, have accents and/or speak quietly

People generally speak a lot quicker than they write. They tend to speak at about 140-160 words per minute though they should be speaking at 120 words per minute (more on this in Chapter 13). If we have someone who talks too fast, has an accent and speaks quietly we're in serious trouble!

Someone once told me that she'd just started working in an organisation and had to take minutes. She hadn't met everyone in the organisation but was surprised in the meeting when they kept talking about a Jamaican. She would've known if she'd met a Jamaican in her pre-dominantly white-European organisation. After the meeting she typed her minutes up and presented them to her manager. Her manager asked her, "What is this Jamaican you have all the way through your minutes?" The lady couldn't explain other that that was what she'd distinctly heard. The manager left the minutes for a while and then the light bulb clicked. It was Jim Aitken not Jamaican. Say Jim Aitken really fast and it sounds like Jamaican.

Solution: Bravery is required here. If you feel it's appropriate, ask the person speaking to slow down and/or speak up.

Listening and writing at the same time

Solution: Keep reading this book to pick up some techniques on good listening skills.

Dual role

Do you have to participate in the meeting while taking the minutes (but hopefully not chair it as well!)? This is a very difficult thing to do, and do well.

Solution: Do one or the other don't do both. Delegate one of your jobs to someone else.

What tools can I use to take minutes?

Solution: See Chapter 7.

The correct template and style to use

Solution: See Chapter 8.

I've never taken minutes before!

Solution: Read the whole book and do all the exercises.

Staying awake and looking interested

I see you nodding and giggling over this one. But seriously, have you ever been in a meeting where the subject was less than exciting or they might as well have been talking in another language (think IT or finance)? Your mind starts to wander. You start to compile a shopping list, think about how much washing needs doing when you get home or what to wear to the barbecue on Saturday night. Then somewhere in the background you hear a voice that brings you back to the present with a jerk. "Did you get that?" someone says. And this is where you nod and vow to sort it out later. This is not a good look.

Solutions:

- Say with a professional voice, "Can you just repeat the last bit?"

- Drink water before and during the meeting to stay hydrated

- Have a good night's sleep before the meeting

- If it's a long meeting, get some fresh air when there's a break. Stand up and walk round

- Eat fruit and nuts to maintain your energy. Avoid too many carbohydrates that make you sleepy.

Summary

There are many challenges for minute takers, but they can all be overcome to varying degrees.

Exercise

Pick two challenges from the list above and write down what you can do to minimise them.

Chapter 2 – Valuing the role of the minute taker

Minute taking is a very important job in organisations, but quite often a task that is undervalued.

I remember working with a woman on a committee where both of us took the minutes. She and I used to joke that before anyone became a committee member it should be compulsory for them to take the minutes for at least a year (we're talking here about meetings that would last two-three days). Why? Because until you've been a minute taker no one really understands what a difficult job it can be.

So let's just do a quick list of what you gain from being a minute taker:

It keeps you informed

If you really want to know what's going on in an organisation, take minutes at a meeting.

You learn more about the organisation or the subject you're minuting

One of the best ways to increase your knowledge is to take minutes.

It keeps your skills current

Do not underestimate the value of a good minute taker. Good minute takers are hard to find and they're highly sought after (mainly because everyone else has chickened out and hasn't developed this skill).

It gets you visible and noticed

If you're taking minutes at high-level meetings you're schmoozing with the movers and shakers in your organisation. This is an opportunity to showcase your skills amongst influential thinkers (and you never know, you may get shoulder-tapped for your dream job).

Summary

Value your role as a minute taker and be proud of what you do. It's a tough job, but you'll learn heaps, and increase your skills and knowledge.

Exercise

Write down two things that you will gain from being a minute taker.

Chapter 3 – Skills required to be a good minute taker

There are lots of skills required to be a good minute taker namely:

- Listening

- Assertiveness

- Organisational ability

- Knowledge of the organisation and subject

- Initiative

- Good command of the written language – spelling, grammar and punctuation, plus the ability to wordsmith sentences into logical and readable paragraphs.

All of the above are important, but the number one skill you need is to be:

A sound, critical thinker

This means having the ability to be able to sift through the information and work out what really needs to be written down.

Now there is such a thing as what I call the LAW of minute taking and it goes like this:

L - Listen

A - Analyse

W - Write

Proactive minute takers will listen, analyse and write. That's the direction we need to be aiming for. However, reactive minute takers will listen, write and analyse (if you're a book writer you'll know what I mean!). Now if you tend to do the latter, tell me if this sounds like you: *I don't know what's important. Everything sounds important. I'm too scared I'm going to miss something so I'll just write everything down and sort it out later.* Sound familiar? And later normally means after the meeting.

There's nothing wrong with doing it that way (and is probably the best approach if you're a new minute taker or unsure of the subject) except you'll be writing down copious amounts of information. This means you'll have a right time-consuming task after the meeting to read through your notes and pull out the essential stuff.

So we want to focus on doing the analyse at the meeting because if you do that you're going to save yourself an awful lot of time afterwards and the process won't be so painful!

Summary

Good minute takers will Listen, Analyse and then Write.

Exercise

Are you a proactive minute taker or a reactive minute taker?

If you're reactive minute taker write down:

- why you think you take your minutes that way, and
- one thing that you could do to become a more proactive minute taker (if you're not sure, don't worry, read on!).

If you're a proactive minute taker, keep doing what you're doing.

Chapter 4 – Developing an effective relationship between the chairman and minute taker

NB: I use the word chairman because it's the correct term to use for this role regardless of gender.

A minute taker's role is much more than just turning up to a meeting and taking the minutes. While, without a doubt, it's the chairman's job to run the meeting the minute taker's subtle influence can have a huge impact on its success.

What can the minute taker do to make the job easier for both themselves and the chairman?

Before the meeting

Prepare a draft agenda together

The basis for the agenda is the minutes from the previous meeting, action points that need to be reviewed, and upcoming items to be discussed.

Set up a briefing meeting with the chairman

The day before, if time permits, meet with the chairman to review the distributed agenda and note any changes. Sometimes it's also a good way to find out about any contentious issues or be given a heads-up on potential outcomes of items or even possible reactions from meeting members.

During the meeting

Sit beside the chairman

Hopefully the days are long gone when the minute taker sat at a separate desk and was never seen or heard from. If you sit beside the chairman you can help control the meeting (in some instances you may end up running the meeting!).

Keep an eye on the time

Sometimes the agenda item being discussed starts to run away and before long the meeting is in danger of falling behind time. In meetings where I've had a good relationship with the chairman I would often point to the agenda when time was ticking away. A simple acknowledgement nod from the chairman was enough for me to know that he (or she) had received my 'times up' message.

This is also a good tactic to use when the meeting has digressed from the agenda.

While the above is really something the chairman should be controlling they sometimes get caught up in the discussions, become distracted and lose track of time. This is where the minute taker can perform a vital back-stop function.

Food's up!

Always a welcome interruption when the minute taker advises that food has arrived and everyone can have a break (yay!).

What do I write down?

This is such an important part of being a successful minute taker that it has its own dedicated chapter (Chapter 5).

After the meeting

Debrief with the chairman

This is an opportunity for you and the chairman to review how the meeting went and whether either of you could do something better next time.

This is also the time where you can ask any questions about anything you were unsure of to clarify the minutes.

Review the draft minutes

After you've typed up your first draft, email your minutes to the chairman for his/her review. Keep on their toes! Chairmen are busy people and reviewing minutes may not be high on their list of priorities, but it's important the minutes are distributed to everyone as soon as possible after the meeting.

Who's responsible for following up on actions?

Make sure you have a clear understanding as to whose job this is. Is your responsibility only to get the action points distributed or are you required to follow up with people to ensure their actions have been completed before the next meeting?

Prepare a draft-draft agenda for the next meeting

This is something you may not necessarily work on with the chairman, but I always found it helpful to get a draft-draft agenda underway while things were still fresh in my mind. It provides a good starting point for preparing the draft agenda (see Before the meeting).

Summary

The three simple tasks of getting that heads-up before the meeting, being the right-hand person and ensuring all the necessary tasks have been completed after the meeting will go a long way to assist in building an effective relationship between the minute taker-and chairman. Always.

Exercise

Write down three things that you can do to foster a more effective relationship with your chairman.

Chapter 5 – The secret to minute taking

OK, so this is the most important chapter in the book.

The secret to minute taking lies with the chairman.

There are many skills required to chair a meeting such as keeping the meeting on track (ie following the agenda), leadership, and subject and meeting knowledge.

The number one skill required of a chairman that will assist the minute taker is to **summarise at the end of each agenda item.**

And this is the secret. If your chairman summarised, would you be able to produce better minutes? Without a doubt, yes. Unfortunately it's something that the majority of chairmen don't do. Why? There are a number reasons, but the main one is that a bit like minute takers they've never had any formal training and so they learn by burn. A lot of chairmen actually believe it's the minute taker's job to summarise. Nope. It's the chairman's job.

Have you ever been taking the minutes, there's been quite a lot of discussion about something and then wham! They've moved onto the next agenda item and you're left thinking…, *So?* There was a lot of discussion, there were some suggestions, but nothing was resolved and things were kind of left hanging. This is where the danger lies because when you go to write the minutes up you'll then have to use your own interpretation and perception of what you think has happened which could be right, but could also be wrong. This puts a lot of responsibility onto the minute taker and really isn't good enough. There should be some kind of closure for every agenda item.

When the chairman summarises it's not just for you, but for everyone else in the meeting as well so they all leave knowing exactly what was agreed to.

Now, how do you get the chairman to summarise? Review Chapter 4 and there are some very specific points are coming up in Chapter 10.

Quite often a question I get asked on my course is, "If the chairman doesn't summarise is it OK for me to ask him/her to do so?" The answer is yes, but this does have to be done with some delicacy. Egos are involved here! If you don't have the confidence to do so or you think it's inappropriate, don't do it. However, if you think that your prompting will be met with support then you could use the following statements:

- "What would you like me to record?"

- "How would you like me to minute that?"

- "Could you please provide me with a summary?"

- "The outcome was...?" (This is a bit cheeky, but one I use when I know the group really well and that I know I can get away with it.)

If chairmen are learning by burning then I believe we, as minute takers, have an obligation to teach them that good summarising is an essential part of a well-run meeting. And if you can get your chairman to summarise at least half of the challenges outlined in Chapter 1 will be solved.

I firmly believe that minutes can only be as good as the person chairing the meeting allows. Think of the meetings you've been to – what made them good meetings? They were well-run, kept to time, had good leadership **and** the chairman summarised. Not so good meetings – disorganised, went over time and you were left in the dark as to what were the key points that needed minuting.

Summary

A good chairman will summarise at the end of each agenda item which will help ensure that the minute taker has recorded the key points.

Exercise

Write down what steps you could take to help you work with your particular chairman to ensure that s/he is summarising (if you're not sure, flick over to Chapter 10).

Chapter 6 – Different purposes and types of meetings

Why do we need to have minutes?

We need minutes because they:

- Provide a historical record

- Provide a record of the discussion

- Provide a record of future action

Sometimes I hear minute takers complain that their minutes never get read. It may feel that way, but don't believe it.

I was delivering a minute taking training course for a city council a number of years ago. It just so happened that on the day of the course, the front page of the local newspaper featured an article about how the council had to go back through sets of minutes from fifty years ago to find out what agreement had been made between the council and a farmer over the use of some land. So you never know when the minutes you took will provide valuable information in the future.

Different types of meetings - Formal and Informal – What's the difference?

A minute taker needs to be able to take minutes at all types of meetings. Meetings generally fall into two groups – formal and informal though there is another group, semi-formal, which is a hybrid of the two.

It is important to know the difference between these meetings because that will depend on what type of minutes you take.

Formal meetings (usually committees, boards or groups, AGMs, shareholder)

A formal meeting will have the following characteristics:

Documentation

There will be a formalised agenda and supporting papers.

Minutes

People quite often use this word loosely: "Can you take minutes at our meeting?" And without thinking about it, that's exactly what we do. But the term minutes should be used only for formal meetings.

Consequently the presentation of the minutes will be in a more structured style using proper sentences and formal language.

Defined roles

People take on defined roles in a meeting: chairman, executive officer, company secretary, minute taker etc.

Formalised decision making

This may be done through the process of a motion being moved, seconded and voted on.

Governing documents

There are a number of documents that detail policies, processes and procedures for formal meetings. Some of these are called standing orders, rules, trust deeds, constitutions and - more commonly - terms of reference. It's important for the minute taker to know whether there is any such documentation for their meeting and be familiar with their contents.

Quorum

Does your formal meeting have a quorum? Hint: check your documentation. Most do, and it's the job of the chairman to ensure that there is a quorum before the meeting starts and that the quorum remains in place throughout the meeting.

I have been in meetings where the chairman has gone to start the meeting and I've had to point out that a quorum wasn't present. I've been surprised a number of times when the chairman has replied they weren't sure what the number was. This is a good chance for the minute taker to show that they know the documentation, which will do great things for your credibility!

Language

Yes, there could be some language! This relates to the proper terms that people may use in meetings eg addressing the chairman as such, asking another member a question "through the chair", or other formal meeting language such as "point of order".

Higher expectations

There is a higher expectation at a formal meeting that the minute taker will take down accurate information and summarise the discussion. This means that the heat is on for you to perform, and as a consequence the stress levels can be higher!

Informal meetings (usually staff catch ups, progress updates or brainstorming)

Agenda

I'm a big believer that every meeting no matter how informal, should have an agenda. An agenda keeps everyone focused and on task and will signpost the discussion. Have you ever been in a meeting where there wasn't an agenda? Did the discussion ramble and go off track?

Notes

This is the big difference for informal meetings. Remember the term 'minutes'? If it's an informal meeting you're more likely to take notes or even just action points, the language will be more informal and the structure and style of the minutes maybe looser.

As a contract minute taker, when I was working with new clients I always asked them if they wanted me to take minutes or notes. This put the onus back on the client to make the decision and removes the responsibility from me in case I ended up taking formal minutes that weren't required or notes when they wanted something more official.

Decisions made by consensus

Decision making in informal meetings tends to be a bit looser where everyone just says "yes" and it's done!

Less structured...

Minute takers tend to prefer informal meetings because they're more relaxed and less stressed. However, such meetings can lose their structure very quickly if they aren't controlled properly. This is mostly likely to happen when there isn't an actual chairman, just a facilitator.

Before you know it the meeting has gone off track and the minute taker (or should that be note taker?) is wondering whether the discussion is worth minuting.

...which allows for more discussion and is more flexible

This is generally a good thing since this kind of forum allows for that all important free-flowing discussion, and we do need flexibility if the discussion goes off track yet is covering something important.

Summary

Knowing the differences between formal and informal meetings and what their characteristics are will help to ensure you're properly prepared, and will be able to display your knowledge by using the most appropriate format – minutes or notes.

Exercise

Write down all the meetings you take minutes for and next to them write whether you think they're formal or informal.

Now think about whether you're using the correct term and format– minutes or notes.

Chapter 7 – Tools to record minutes

Writing

Formalised shorthand

Many years ago it would've been unheard of for a secretary not to have been trained in Pitmans or Teeline Shorthand. Probably because of the invention of technology shorthand has become a dying art. It makes me feel old when the millennials who attend my course have no idea what I'm talking about.

If you'd like to know a little bit more about Pitmans or Teeline Shorthand pop on over to www.teelineshorthand.org or www.long-live-pitmans-shorthand.org.uk.

There's also Easyscript at www.easyscript.com.

Informal shorthand

Millennials will know what this is all about – texting. Despite what your opinions maybe about texting it's a great way to abbreviate down words ie:

Im sr u wil hv no trbl n rdg ths

So what exactly is texting? It's a combination of using just vowels (u instead of you) or taking the vowels out (rdg for reading).

In conjunction with texting you can use other shortforms and abbreviations. I have compiled a list which you may find helpful and you can download it at https://minutesmadness.wordpress.com/free-resources/.

It doesn't matter what you use as long as the words are as compact as possible, and - probably more importantly - you can read your writing later!

Highlighter

Take a highlighter pen to meetings. Highlight the main points when someone is speaking to a written report. Then after the meeting copy the highlighted bits into the minutes. This saves time and it means you're not writing/typing stuff down that's already there.

Lap-top

If you're a fast typist this is definitely the way to go.

The beauty of typing the minutes straight into the lap top is that, theoretically, at the end of the meeting all you have to do is a cut and paste, a spell check and a tidy up and – voila! – the minutes are done.

Also, before the meeting you can load your meeting template into the lap top with all the bits and pieces pre-filled out.

I know some minute takers who, after using a lap top, have had to revert back to pen and paper because people in the meeting have complained about the tapping on the keys. Really? I don't think it's a big issue and surely if people are talking this is masking the sound of the typing? I've never had a problem and I think that with all the technology available to us these days it's just expected that a lap top is something that will be used. However, I don't envy the very few minute takers who use a lap top that projects up the minutes onto a datashow. Talk about pressure!

A couple of tips when using lap tops:

• Take a pen and paper in case of a technological catastrophe!

- Make sure the battery is fully powered.

- Ensure you turn the power switch on when plugging in your lap top (I've forgotten to occasionally – duh!)

- Work off-line

- If borrowing a lap top make sure you're really familiar with it before using it

- If you find the keyboard too small, plug in your regular size one

- Set Auto-Save to every five minutes minimum

- Save in two places – hard drive and USB

- Set up Auto Correct for common words that you type so you don't have to type them in full

- If you're distracted by the squiggly error lines, turn your spell checker off

iPads

Fiddly things (use a wireless keyboard), but I'm seeing more and more minute takers using these.

The following apps have been recommended as good ones to use:

Evernote:

https://itunes.apple.com/nz/app/evernote-capture-notes-sync/id281796108?mt=8

Notability:

https://itunes.apple.com/nz/app/notability/id360593530?mt=8

Just a word of caution: Be careful about using apps that haven't been recommended to you. A lot of apps have been developed by hobbyists and still have a lot of rats and mice in them and you don't want your app to let you down in the middle of a meeting.

Recording devices

I encourage minute takers not to use recording devices because you can end up relying on it too much. It's a good tool to use when you're first taking minutes and are unsure of the subject, but it should only be used to clarify something. I've had some minute takers admit that they've taken minutes at the meeting, recorded it as well and then after the meeting listened to the whole recording again. Painful!

Also you do need to be aware that you must ask people's permission before you record them.

If you want a really cool recording device check out https://www.smartpen.co.nz/

Summary

The main tools to use to take minutes are: pen and paper, highlighter, laptop or iPad or recording devices.

Whether you write or use a lap top is a matter of personal choice but if you're a fast typist I encourage you to have a go.

For some people they can't use a lap top because there isn't one available. I encourage you to beg, steal or borrow one because it will save you a heap of time. If you're writing your minutes you're double handling the information.

Exercise

Think about how you're taking the minutes. Could you take them in a more efficient way?

Chapter 8 – Minute templates – it's a jungle out there!

If you're a seasoned minute taker, you'll know that how the minutes are presented will go a long way towards their readability.

I get asked a lot of questions on my minute-taking courses round what would be a good template to use.

The first thing is to find out whether your organisation has a preferred template, and if there is one, of course, this should be used.

If there's no prescribed template, you can use whatever you like. However, there are a couple of things to think about:

- Is the meeting I'm taking minutes at formal or informal?
- How much information will I need to be putting in my template?
- Who is my audience?

I've gathered together eight minute templates which are pretty much the standard these days. These templates, with a description of each, are available at https://minutesmadness.wordpress.com/free-resources/. I hope you find them helpful!

Summary

Ensure that you're using a template that suits the meeting type.

Exercise

Review the templates you're currently using. Do they suit your meetings? Which ones from the free resources could you use for your meetings or adapt to suit purpose?

Chapter 9 – Styles of minutes

In this chapter we'll look at three different styles of minutes.

Have a read of the three examples that follow and jot down your thoughts about the different styles.

Example 1

Use of the Customer Feedback Forms

The CEO stated that a discussion was required to take place on the decrease in the customer feedback forms being received.

Mr Bloggs said he would like the system to continue.

Mrs Smith agreed.

Mr Goal stated he also agreed, but felt that there needed to be more promotion.

Mr Bloggs suggested that a reward be given for the best feedback.

It was agreed that the reward be a dinner voucher to be used in the restaurant to the value of $50.

It was agreed that the unit manager make the presentation to the customer who had the best feedback.

The CEO wanted to be informed when presentations took place.

It was also agreed that suggestions made after 31 August would be eligible for the reward.

It was also agreed that this be mentioned at the next staff meeting. New customer feedback forms would be printed and the winning customer would also be profiled on Facebook and any other social media avenues as appropriate. This needed to be actioned by Friday.

Your thoughts:

My thoughts: Painful, huh? The minute taker has made no attempt to summarise these minutes. S/he has written down exactly what was said, who said it and probably in exactly the order it was said at the meeting. The reader has to do a lot of work here; they have to read the whole story (or soap opera as one person described it) to work out what happened and what has to be done.

These minutes are called *narrative* or *verbatim minutes* (as said, or word for word). It also uses the "he said, she said" format.

This is an old-fashioned style and there has been a complete move away from this over the years.

You may recognise this style as one that you used when you first started taking minutes. So if you're new to minute taking, the above example is a good example of what not to do.

Important Point No. 1

Minutes should record what was said - ie content - and not who said it. As much as you possibly can avoid using people's names in minutes such as in the above example (more on this below). Don't attribute comments with names.

Important Point No. 2

There are generally only two times you would use names:

- When someone introduces a subject and in this case I would use their title eg *The CEO provided a background as to why there would be budget cuts this year* or

- When a person has to do something ie an action point eg *Lyn will follow this up in time for the next meeting.*

There are two reasons for not using names. The main one is that if you put a person's name in the minutes along with their comments you put that person and your organisation at legal risk. Minutes can be used as evidence in court, and you want to minimise all risk by ensuring that your minutes are a summarised version of the discussion without using names.

The other reason is that most boards, groups, committees etc prefer themselves to be seen as collective in their decision making rather than individual names standing out in lights. Discussions therefore can be minuted by saying, *The Board agreed..., The Board commented...*

There have been times when I have felt it warranted to attribute a comment to a name. In one particular meeting the financial officer was making it very clear to the committee that if they took a particular course of action then there could be consequences. The committee made a decision that went against the financial officer's advice and I thought it was important to make sure (just in case it came back to bite him later) that he had given this advice. The comment I wrote in the minutes was: *The financial officer advised against this course of action because...*

Most of the time we don't need to know who said something, but if you're unsure whether you should be using people's names the question to ask yourself is: *Will it be relevant for people to know who said this?*

Verbatim minutes do have their uses and are quite often used in court-like settings eg hearings and will also be used in disciplinary or personal grievance meetings when it's important to know exactly what was said and who said it.

Example 2

Use of the Customer Feedback Forms

A discussion took place on the decrease in the number of customer feedback forms being received.

There was consensus as to continuing the system in principle, but agreement that there needed to be more promotion.

In order to encourage suggestions, a discussion took place on giving a reward for the best feedback offered.

It was agreed that the reward be a dinner voucher to be used in the restaurant to the value of $50.

It was agreed that the unit manager would make the presentation to the customer who had the best feedback. It was thought that the CEO should also be informed.

Suggestions made after 31 August would be eligible for the reward.

It was also agreed that this be mentioned at the next staff meeting. New customer feedback forms would be printed and the winning customer would also be profiled on Facebook and any other social media avenues as appropriate. This needed to be actioned by Friday.

Your thoughts:

My thoughts: Better than Example 1? Notice the names have been removed. However, you still have to read the whole thing through.

This type of minutes is what I call *Summary minutes using the three step approach*.

Step 1 - First paragraph – Background.

Step 2 - Second to fifth paragraph – Discussion.

Step 3 - Sixth to seventh paragraph – Result.

These are good steps to follow to structure your minutes within a particular agenda item.

Example 3

Discussion/Decision/Action	Responsibility	Timeframe
1. Use of Customer Feedback forms A discussion took place on the decrease in the number of customer feedback forms being received. It was agreed: <ul><li>to continue the system in principal, but agreement that there needed to be more promotion</li><li>to offer a reward of a $50 dinner voucher to be used in the restaurant</li><li>the unit manager make the presentation to the customer who had the best feedback and that the CEO be informed</li><li>suggestions made after 31 August would be eligible for the payment</li><li>new customer feedback forms to be printed and the winning customer profiled on Facebook and other social media</li></ul>	Unit Mgr.	5 August

These are what we call *action-point minutes* and this is by far the most popular style used today.

The table format allows ease of readability for the reader with its clear columns. The discussion has been summarised, names have been eliminated and bullet points have been used. Bullet points are great for writing. Our eye automatically focuses on the bullet point, we tend to use fewer words and it creates white space. The more white space you have in a document the easier it is to read.

Summary

Minutes should record content; be sure to minimise use of names in your minutes.

The best type of minute style to use for most meetings is action-point minutes.

Exercise

Which style are you currently using? Is this the best style for your meetings?

Review your last two sets of minutes. How often did you use names? Can you rewrite these parts without naming people?

Chapter 10 – Top three tips for writing minutes

Minutes need to be clear, concise and condensed and the following are my top three tips on how to do that:

Tip No. 1

Write the minutes from the point of view of someone who did not attend the meeting.

This is a good test to do. Once you've finished your draft minutes take one step back (literally!) and re-read your minutes as if you weren't at the meeting. What you're looking for are two things:

- Have I put too much unnecessary information in my minutes (this is particularly relevant for those book writers out there)? or

- Have I not put enough information in my minutes?

I always apply this test every time I do a set of minutes and I'll either end up adding some information to clarify something or take information out because it was unnecessary.

When I've worked with management and the subject of meetings and minutes arises I take the chance to ask them what they define as a good set of minutes? Every time this answer comes back: If I wasn't at the meeting I should be able to read the minutes without having to plough through a book.

Tip No. 2

Record 'need to know' not 'nice to know'. Other words for nice to know are: irrelevant, inconsequential, waffle, fluff, gossip, and scandal. Now, remember the LAW from Chapter 3? Listen, Analyse, Write. This is the first time in a meeting you should start to apply this technique. So instead of being that reactive minute taker who writes everything down, now you're going to analyse what you're hearing and think *Is what I'm hearing need to know or nice to know?* This way you'll start to write down only the pertinent points.

Tip No. 3

Use the three step approach to recording a discussion (Chapter 9) or the DART technique.

The DART technique is as follows:

D iscussion – Record the summarised discussion only (ie no "he said/she said") plus also think about, *Why is this issue important? Why is it so important we have to have a meeting about it?*

D ecisions – Self-explanatory.

D eferred items – This relates to anything that can't be addressed at the meeting. The heads-up for this are words or phrases such as, *Let's defer this, Let's take this off-line, Let it lie on the table, Let's put this on the backburner.* Minute takers need to listen out for these and capture them in the minutes because if you don't the item will get forgotten about.

A ctions – What is to be done.

R esponsibilities – Who's going to do it.

T imeframe - When it's going to get done.

Most meetings will have quite a lot of discussion and hopefully some decisions are being made, but have you ever noticed things quite often stop there? What happens when there's no responsibility allocated to an action? Nothing will get done. And if a person is allocated a job, but there's no timeframe? It will never get done!

By using the DART technique in your minutes you'll be ensuring that you're capturing the key components.

Now remember in Chapter 5 I mentioned I would give you a technique to help not only the chairman but also you to summarise. This is it!

When you've finished reading this chapter mention to the chairman – as long as you think it's appropriate - that what will help you get better minutes is if they could summarise at the end of each agenda item. Most chairmen will be happy to oblige. The fun starts when you're actually in the meeting. How do you ensure they'll follow through on their promise? Remember the briefing meeting you'll have with the chairman before the meeting? This is where you can give them a subtle reminder that they'll be summarising. However, in full-flight of the meeting it's easy for them to forget. This is what I suggest you do:

Type up the DART technique onto coloured paper. Take it with you to the meeting and have it sitting beside you and the chairman so when s/he starts to move off the agenda item and they haven't summarised you can point at the piece of paper.

Hopefully the chairman will then say, "OK, everyone, we've just had a discussion on XXX. The main points were XXX. The decision is XXX. This is what will happen (action) XXX. XXX (name of person) is going to do it and the timeframe will be XXX." How cool would that be?

Trending

Over the years there has been a trend that overall has been a good one. Management are now instructing minute takers to record only actions. Whoo hoo! That's great because it saves you a tonne of work. Now this suits a certain type of meeting, mainly the informal type. It's not so good for formal meetings and this is because a lot of formal meeting minutes will be audited. What auditors will be looking for is whether there is enough information that shows how a decision was reached. So it's not enough to just write the decision - you have to include a little bit about options, points, scenarios etc that were considered and that led to the decision.

Summary

- Write clear, concise and condensed minutes.

- Write the minutes from the point of view of someone who didn't attend the meeting.

- Write down only information that people need to know.

- Use the DART technique.

Exercise

Make a note to talk to the chairman in the briefing meeting about the DART technique.

Type up the DART technique onto coloured paper.

Modify your minute template so it has the DART headings on it.

Chapter 11 – Determining what needs to be recorded – Part 1

Determining what needs to be recorded is another way of saying *How do I work out the key points versus the waffle?*

There are two ways to do this. This chapter will focus on being selective.

Be selective

Exercise

Below are some questions/statements that may or may not be important to consider when deciding whether to minute something in a meeting. Decide whether each of the following is a 'yes' or a 'no'.

Should I:

- Write everything down?
- Ask myself, "Is this issue/point/comment important to note?"
- Consider whether including this information would help someone understand the issue being discussed.
- Consider whether there is there any value in writing this information.
- Ask myself, "Have I already written this point down?"
- Consider whether this is a new point.

Did you mark everything with a yes except the first one? If you did, you've scored six out of six!

Let's put a bit of detail round some of the above points.

Don't write everything down

Avoid writing everything down because the more detail you put in your minutes the more likely you're to get it wrong. A good thing to remember: *Listen more and write less.* Less is best.

Consider whether there is any value in writing this information

When someone says something in a meeting do they think what they've said is of any value? Yep, otherwise they wouldn't have said anything! But this is where the power of the minute taker lies. This is where you get to decide whether what that person said was of any value. So when people are talking in a meeting I'm constantly asking myself, *Is what that person saying important?* You only have a split second to make that decision. Usually I can do it within that split second. Sometimes I'm dithering, unable to make up my mind. Now the tricky bit is that while you're doing your dither, they're not waiting for you - they're moving on. So if 'value' isn't working for me I get a bit flippant and think, *So what?* And when I think *So what?* it always tips me over to making a decision.

Have I already written this point down?

Do you sometimes feel like if you're not writing the whole time in a meeting you're not doing your job? Or you get the glare?

Another part of analysing is to be constantly thinking as to whether you've already written a point down that is now being said in different words. Regardless of how many times something has been said at a meeting, regardless of who's said it you need to write the comment down only once. Simple. Saves a lot of time.

How do people make decisions in meetings? They do this by discussion. And this discussion can go on and on and on... while everyone feels they have to add their bit. The minute taker needs to listen carefully. Note down points as they arise, but if a comment is repeated don't write it down again, because you've already written it down! If it's said once, write it once.

And remember, your job is to summarise the minutes so all the comments people are saying will be written down only once in your minutes because you're not using, "he said/she said".

Putting it all together

All of the above points under Be Selective are what we need to do if we're analysing. Now I'm not suggesting that you memorise the points and apply it every time someone speaks because by the time you've remembered them the meeting might've moved on and you won't have written anything down. So the three things I use in a meeting are:

- Need to know versus nice to know

- Is there any value?

- Have I already written it down?

I'll guarantee that if you use those three phrases you won't have time to think about your shopping list!

How to quickly record different viewpoints

Meetings often allow for the discussion of certain subjects where the following aspects need to be considered:

- Advantages versus disadvantages

- Pluses and minuses

- Pros and cons

Sometimes there may be different viewpoints to the subject being discussed and they aren't all said in a nice structured way.

Imagine being a minute taker who works for a library. You're in a meeting and the agenda item that is about to be discussed is replacing books with e-readers. Not only is this a pretty big issue, it's also full of emotion.

It's likely that the following issues will arise:

- Loss of librarian jobs
- More eco-friendly
- More portable
- Less non-fiction available
- Costs – licenses, purchase, maintenance, upgrades etc
- No waiting lists
- Breaks more easily
- Non-usable if dropped in water
- Dual purpose
- Smaller
- More private (you can now read Fifty Shades of Grey and no one will know!)
- Theft
- Alienates some parts of the community
- Encourages younger readers
- Constant upgrading
- Can increase font size

- Cheaper to buy books

- Stable market

- More space in the library

The minute taker probably wrote these down as they were said, which is OK, but the hard bit comes after the meeting when you have to sort through the list and get them into some kind of logical order.

Let's rewind back to the meeting.

Instead of the minute taker writing down the points of view as they were said, how about they follow what I call the division of two (or however many) alternatives?

If you're typing your minutes directly onto a lap top use the table function or you can simply tab. If you're handwriting, divide your page into two parts and head up each column with an appropriate heading.

Now as the comments at the meeting are made you then insert them into the appropriate column.

Here is an example of the completed exercise:

E-readers versus books

A discussion took place on the merits of replacing books with e-readers:

Advantages	Disadvantages
More eco-friendly	Loss of librarian jobs
More portable	Less non-fiction available
No waiting lists	Cost – licenses, purchase,
Dual Purpose	maintenance, upgrades, etc.
Smaller	Breaks more easily
More private (You can read Fifty	Non-usable if dropped in water
Shades of Grey and no one will	Theft
ever know!)	Alienates some parts of the
Encourages younger readers	community
Can increase font size	Constant upgrading
Stable market	
More space in the library	

If you use the division of two alternatives it means that after the meeting – voila! - you already have your viewpoints summarised nicely into a logical order.

Summary

Listen more, write less.

Even If it's said more than once, write it once.

Exercise

Pick one of the points from the Be Selective list.

At your next meeting concentrate on that particular point - eg you might focus on not writing everything down or it could be deciding whether what you're hearing is of any value.

Chapter 12 - Checkpoint

How are we doing?

Let's review the tips we've covered:

- Good minute takers will: Listen, Analyse, Write.

- Minutes should record content only; be sure to minimise the use of names in your minutes.

- Write clear, concise and condensed minutes.

- Write the minutes from the point of view of someone who didn't attend the meeting.

- Write down only information that is need to know.

- Use the DART technique.

- Listen more, write less.

- If it's said once, write it once.

Are you ready to have a go at turning some verbatim minutes into a nice set of action point minutes?

Exercise

Rewrite these minutes into action-point minutes.

Meeting attendees

Karen (chairman), Sue, Lorraine

Purchase of an electronic whiteboard

Sue said there had been some suggestions from personal assistants that what people were writing on a whiteboard during meetings could be electronically photocopied off and that we should look at purchasing an electronic whiteboard.

Karen replied that it would be quite an expense, given that the administration budget is already over.

Lorraine commented that we would need to look at the advantages and disadvantages first before making a decision.

Sue said that she'd done some research. WBC Ltd sold electronic whiteboards for $1,000.

Karen thought the advantages would need to be discussed in more detail.

Sue felt that an electronic whiteboard would be warranted. She was quite often in meetings taking minutes for the veterinarians who put up complicated diagrams on the whiteboard and expected her to be able to take them down perfectly. Having the exact example of what was written would be great.

Lorraine agreed. She sometimes couldn't get down all the information before it was wiped off. The electronic whiteboard would be able to print it off immediately, give her a copy and then everyone could move onto the next subject without wasting time.

Sue commented that you could also return to the writing on the other side of the whiteboard by using the forward key.

Karen asked about the disadvantages. She'd used whiteboards in the past and they were always breaking down.

Sue said there was a particular model a couple of years ago that there was a specific problem with, but she thought it had been fixed.

Lorraine thought that there was a certain brand you couldn't get parts for anymore.

Karen suggested that a site visit takes place to one of the office suppliers so they could see some whiteboards. She also pointed out one problem with whiteboards is that no one ever keeps paper nearby and you have to go and get paper to load into the machine and that wastes time.

Sue wondered whether the whiteboard would fit in the lift if it was required to be moved between floors. A whiteboard needs power too.

Lorraine replied that you can still copy the information off the board. You just wouldn't be able to print if off.

Karen thought that we should purchase a whiteboard from WBC Ltd.

Lorraine supported the idea of doing a site visit. Then they could see the whiteboards, get a demonstration and ask questions.

Sue was happy to do this. She asked if people could e-mail her some dates when they were available.

Ends.

How'd you go? A suggested model answer follows.

1. Purchasing an electronic whiteboard • There have been some suggestions from the PA's to purchase an electronic whiteboard. • It was noted that this would be expensive given that the administration is already over budget • A discussion took place on the advantages and disadvantages of purchasing an electronic whiteboard **Advantages** More accurate recording of diagrams Immediate printout which saves time Two sides **Disadvantages** Maintenance Consumables Portability Needs power • WBC Ltd sell electronic whiteboards for $1,000 plus GST • It was agreed that: * A site visit will be arranged * Suitable dates for site visits to be emailed to S. Saunders	 SS All

Chapter 13 – Determining what needs to be recorded – Part 2

Minute takers need to be able to paraphrase. The Oxford dictionary defines the word paraphrase as, *express the meaning of a passage in other words.*

How do we paraphrase?

Some tips follow:

Listen out for key words

Exercise

Ask someone to read out the following paragraph at a comfortable speed for you, and take down what you believe to be the key points.

Mr Dodds advised he had spoken to Tania regarding the essay competition. It is currently being changed to Year 11. Tania is very enthusiastic about this and suggested that it be done for all design schools with a local institution providing sponsorship. The essays could be published. It could also be extended Australasia wide. It would not be expensive to do. There would be a need to look at how to assign the topics. The polytech would devise the topics and the students choose one. Essay length would be strictly enforced being no more than 1,500 words. The objective of the essay would be on current building design issues using recycled materials. The prize would be approximately $1,000.

Did you manage to get it all down?

Your notes might've looked something like this:

- SA comp

- Chngd 2 Yr 11

- Al dsgn schls

- Lcl inst 2 prv s/hp

- Publ

- Aust[a]→

- Nxspnsv

- Poly dvs tpc stnt chos 1

- 1500 wrds max

- Obj – cnt bldg dsgn isus usg rcycld mats

- Prz – aprox $1k

Now have a look at how you wrote your notes. What did you write in full that could've been written in a shorter form? Did you write sponsorship out in full? What about the $1k? Did you write $1,000 instead? By reducing down the number of characters you write you'll be able to keep up more easily. If you think you need to, go back and review Chapter 7.

Filter out glue words

Glue words, or conjunctions, are the little words that glue our sentences together eg at, is, be, that, in, is, a.

As a minute taker if you filter out the glue words the key points will become more obvious.

Go back to the exercise and have someone read it out again. Can you hear the glue words? For example (glue words in bold), *Essay length* **would be** *strictly enforced* **being** *no more* **than** *1,500 words.*

Recognise meeting participants' communication styles

A good minute taker will listen and observe as to how people in meetings communicate.

Signal statements

At your next meeting listen out to see if anyone uses signal statements. Signal statements indicate that someone is about to tell you something important. Some examples of signal statements are:

- The most important point is...

- What I'm concerned about ...

- What I want to know is ...

- I think we need to...

- I strongly advise...

- To reiterate...

- In summary...

- What I want to point out is...

- What I'm trying to say is...

- For the minutes...

- Basically... (another word for summary)

- Going forward... (such a cliché, but what comes next is hopefully a suggested course of action)

- At the end of the day... (ditto)

One participant in a meeting I took minutes for always used to start what he wanted to say with something like, "In 1974..." and then he'd proceed to give everyone a whole lot of detail, which always sounded really important. So here I was minuting this down on my lap top. I would time him and the minimum amount of time it would take for him to get out what he wanted to say was seven minutes. A long time to be typing. But one day the light bulb went off in my head. I realised that round about the six-minute mark he would say something like, "So what I'm concerned about is..." or "So what I want to know is..." and then he'd get to the point. When did I actually have to start typing? Yep, at the six-minute mark. All I had to do was listen out for his signal statements.

Should I mention the minute taker who told me that her chairman used to give her a physical signal statement? When her eyes had glazed over (obviously an unexciting meeting) he used to slap the table between the two of them to bring her back to the meeting!

Where will the main point be?

Listen to people in your meetings. When they speak where is there main point likely to be?

There are only three possible answers:

At the beginning

In the middle

At the end

The three groups of communicators in meetings

I find when people speak in meetings they generally fall into three main groups. And every meeting will have at least one of these:

The dark horse

These are the meeting participants who very rarely say anything, but when they do it's like a profound statement. They choose their times to speak. Their messages are quite often short, sharp, and to the point. They have an amazing ability to suggest a path forward when the group has got stuck on something.

How to minute a dark horse - when they speak, start writing straight away. If you don't, by the time they've said what they've said you might've missed it. Dark horses quite often use eloquent language and their exact words are worth getting down.

The majority

Sorry, no fancy term for these people but this is the group most of us fall into. This group of people's main point comes at the beginning. They then give a whole lot of justification as to why they think that way and as they come to the end of their piece they say again what they said at the start, but may use different words eg I think that we should replace books with e-readers **(main point at the start)** because **(justification)** etc, etc so I support the idea of replacing books with e-readers **(repeats the main point again)**.

How to minute the majority – Pay special attention to their first and last sentence.

Wafflers

OK, so we all know who these people are! These are the people who take ages to get to the point - if there is one. And every meeting seems to have one – or two! These are the hardest group for minute takers to try and understand and to summarise. We listen so carefully for what it is they're trying to say, but everything becomes a whole lot of words. Sound familiar? We just have to do our best to make some kind of sense of what they're saying.

If you've done any study in communication, you'll know that the more accurate term to describe these people is 'auditory'. Auditory people externalise their thinking - ie they think out loud. They have no filters! They love to listen to stories and they're great storytellers. If you know an auditory person they quite often use the phrase, "To cut a long story short…". You may be an auditory person yourself. Hint: If, as you start to speak, anyone you live with, work with or socialise with says, "Is this going to take very long?" – you're auditory! You'll also be more likely to use the signal statement, "What I'm trying to say is…?"

How to minute a waffler – do your best to listen out for a key point.

Listen for the message

It's easy for a minute taker to get lost in the words, or things just get missed in translation.

Minute takers need to be able to listen in a block. What this means is to be able to not write things down as you're hearing them but listen, wait a wee bit until you think you've got the gist of what someone is saying, and then just write down the message. This is quite a difficult skill to master because you don't want to leave it too long in case you lose your grasp of what the person was saying. This takes a sure confidence in your ability to pause, listen for the message and then summarise the discussion.

The best way to practise

Watch the evening news on TV (or on the internet). For each news item that comes on, write some key points down on a notepad. As the news item starts to come to an end you should've been able to write down one sentence that captured the context of the item.

The reason why I suggest the news, can you remember how fast most of us speak? 140-160 words per minute. And we should be speaking at 120 words per minute. Newsreaders are trained to speak at 120 words per minute. Why this magic figure? Studies have shown that it's a good rate of speech for us to hear what's being said and process it while still hearing the next bit. Anything over 120 words per minute and our brains find it very hard to process the information because it's coming at us too fast. Everything then gets lost, scrambled and jumbled. So now we just need to train everyone to speak at 120 words per minute.

Summary

Paraphrasing means:

- Listening out for key words

- Filtering out glue words

- Becoming familiar with meeting participants' communication styles (signal statements, and at what point in their discussion is the main point likely to be)

Exercises

If you can, have someone read out the following statement (or just pretend someone is saying this in a meeting) and see how far you can get before you feel the need to write something down. Can you paraphrase the discussion down into one sentence?

There has been a marked increase in the number of cars in the car park. The car park is now too small. If the car park is full there is nowhere else to park as there are yellow lines outside the store. We are losing customers because of this.

If you came up with something like:

"The size of the car park needs addressing because we are losing customers." - you've done well.

There's a wee bit of a formula to this, as follows:

The size of the car park needs addressing *(state the issue)* because we are losing customers (*why it is an issue*).

***

Now try this one. See if you can capture the message and summarise the following paragraph:

Customers have found the toy box in reception area a great way to ensure their children are entertained and don't get bored while their parents are waiting to see their lawyer.

Chapter 14 – Help! I'm a book writer - the incredibly shrinking notes

OK, so you've read the previous chapters and you've tried some of the suggestions, but do you still feel as though you're taking down too much?

Exercise

Here's a great exercise for you to try:

Step 1

Have a look at some notes that you took at a meeting. Type these up so they take up no more than **one page**.

Example

Here's some raw notes taken at a meeting on interviewing arrangements for the CEO's new personal assistant:

The CEO has asked for two PAs to be on the interviewing panel and that some interviewing questions be devised.

After a discussion it was agreed that skills testing be undertaken to test advanced knowledge of mail merge and PowerPoint (insertion of audio and video clips).

The successful applicant will need an above average knowledge of business writing including drafting correspondence. A high level of spelling, grammar and punctuation will be required.

It was agreed that Mary Summers be asked to prepare mail merge and PowerPoint tests and Carla Bradshaw be asked to prepare spelling, punctuation and grammar tests.

The CEO had requested that the interview be conducted using the competency based interview format. The use of the STAR (Situation, Tactics, Action, Result) technique in compiling and answering interview questions was explained.

After a discussion it was agreed that the following interview questions be forwarded to the CEO for consideration:

Have you seen the job description?

Why are you interested in the position?

What areas professionally would you like to develop to continue your own learning?

How would people describe your interpersonal skills?

Describe a time you were able to anticipate a problem.

How do you manage your time?

It was agreed that the chairman forward these questions to the CEO.

Step 2

Now see if you reduce the above information down to half a page and then check this against the suggested answer.

Suggested answer:

- Two PAs to be on the interviewing panel.

- Skills testing be undertaken to test advanced knowledge of mail merge and PowerPoint (insertion of audio and video clips).

- Successful applicant will need an above average knowledge of business writing including drafting correspondence. A high level of spelling, grammar and punctuation will be required.

- Agreed that Mary Summers be asked to prepare mail merge and PowerPoint tests and Carla Bradshaw be asked to prepare spelling, punctuation and grammar tests.

- CEO had requested that the interview be conducted using the competency based interview format ie the STAR (Situation, Tactics, Action, Result) technique in compiling and answering interview questions was explained.

- Agreed that the following interview questions be forwarded to the CEO for consideration:

  - Have you seen the job description?

  - Why are you interested in the position?

  - What areas would you like to develop to continue your own professional development?

  - How would people describe your interpersonal skills?

  - Describe a time you were able to anticipate a problem.

  - How do you manage your time?

  - Agreed that the chairman forward these questions to the CEO.

Step 3

Now see if you can reduce the information down yet again while still keeping the salient points.

Suggested answer:

- Two PAs to be on the interviewing panel.

- Testing of advanced knowledge of mail merge and PowerPoint (audio and video clips)

- High level of business writing skills required.

- Action: Mary Summers to prepare Microsoft Word and PowerPoint tests and Carla Bradshaw to prepare spelling, punctuation and grammar tests.

- Interview to be conducted using the competency based interview format ie STAR (Situation, Tactics, Action, Result).

- Chairman to forward following questions to the CEO for consideration:

  - Have you seen the job description?

  - Why are you interested in the position?

  - What areas would you like to develop to continue your own professional development?

  - How would people describe your interpersonal skills?

  - Describe a time you were able to anticipate a problem.

  - How do you manage your time?

  - Agreed that the chairman forward these questions to the CEO.

***

How did you go?

Summary

Keep reducing down your notes until you have just the salient points.

Exercise

Take a set of raw notes and see if you can reduce them down twice while still keeping the most important points.

Chapter 15 – Sentence starters and choice words

So you've taken minutes at your meeting and you're now typing them up. The phone has been ringing, your manager has interrupted you twice and your goal was to finish the darn thing before you went home!

You want to keep the momentum going, but you're stuck on how to start sentences. You look back over your magnificent minutes and realise that every sentence starts the same way. Bother!

Below is a list of statements you can use to start those sentences:

Comments made were...

- It was noted... (not to be used too often!)
- It was suggested...
- Concern was expressed...
- It was clarified...
- Key points of discussion noted were...
- Main points were...
- Consideration was given to...
- It's also OK to summarise a long discussion by prefacing one of the above with:
- An extensive discussion took place...
- After considerable discussion...
- A lengthy debate took place...

Don't use, *A healthy and robust discussion took place.* This is a bit of an old phrase, which I still see occasionally in minutes. The picture I see is of a heated discussion that may've got physical!

Also our job as minute takers is to make the minutes look good both presentation wise and with the words that are used.

Below is a list of colloquial words that people have probably used in meetings. These can be smartened up as follows:

- *Drawn up, put together becomes compiled, formulated*
- *Sort out becomes resolved*
- *Done becomes undertaken*
- *Set up becomes established*
- *Look at becomes view*
- *Brought up becomes raised*

Summary

Mix up the way you start your sentences.

Smarten up informal words to make them more professional.

Exercise

Have a look at your last set of minutes. Did you have variety in how your sentences started? Are there any examples from the above that you could have used instead?

Chapter 16 – The most secretive of meetings

There may be times when a meeting will go "in committee" or meetings are conducted under conditions such as "closed", "public excluded", "in house" or "Board only time".

The reason for this is usually to discuss issues that are private, confidential or commercially sensitive and the information shouldn't be out in the public domain. Participants may go in committee part way through a meeting, or there may be a separate part of the meeting that is dedicated to in committee matters.

What should the minute taker be doing?

Make sure you're clear about what your role is at this point. Should you actually be in the meeting? Given the nature of the discussions, it maybe wise for you not to be. If you stay in the meeting, do they want minutes taken? Sometimes the group may just want an off-the-record discussion. At other times the discussion will still need to be minuted. If you're not sure what you should be doing, don't be afraid to ask the chairman.

Separate minutes

If you're required to take the minutes then you need to start a fresh page. At the top of the minutes include the words "In Committee Meeting".

These minutes will be no different to any normal set of minutes in terms of content.

However, in the main set of minutes it needs to be recorded that there was an in committee session eg:

The meeting went in committee at 12.40 pm.

The meeting came out of in committee at 12.50 pm.

It's also a good idea to put a "confidential" watermark on the in committee minutes so everyone who receives them is clear of its status.

Distribution

Generally they'll be emailed, but there's an important thing to remember here: once confidential minutes are emailed out they can then be emailed on to other people.

Approval of minutes

At the next meeting two sets of minutes will need to be approved: the main set and the in committee set.

Filing

If hard copies of the minutes are required to be kept, the in committee minutes should be filed separately from the main minutes and locked away.

Summary

Ensure you know what your role is in an in committee meeting.

Take separate minutes headed up "In Committee Minutes".

Chapter 17 – Minute-taking checklist

Use the following checklist to keep you focused when you're taking minutes:

- Record "need to know" not "nice to know".

- Record issues/points/comments that are important to note.

- Consider whether including particular information would help someone understand the issue being discussed.

- Consider whether there is any value in recording this information.

- Write information once only.

- Record new points.

- Use the division of two alternatives (where appropriate).

- Listen for signal statements.

- Listen for the message.

- And don't write everything down!

Chapter 18 – To summarise...

It's a tough job being a minute taker, but hopefully by the time you've arrived here you'll have been able to practise some of the techniques.

To summarise down to three main points...

- Work with your chairmen and train them to summarise at the end of each agenda item. Honestly, this will change your life!

- Remember the LAW – Listen, Analyse, Write.

- Use the DART technique – Record discussions, deferred items and decisions; note actions, responsibilities and timeframes.

If you succeed you will go a long way to writing clear, concise and condensed minutes and still keep your sanity!

I wish you all be best in the mad world of minute taking.

Acknowledgements

Many thanks to the following people. I couldn't have done it without you.

Lesley Marshall - for providing valuable editorial suggestions.

Lynn O'Shea - for designing the awesome cover.

Tendai Nyamdela and Sherie Pointon - for providing an honest review of content.

Shifan Mohamed Rizmie – for providing valuable advice on manuscript preparation and formatting for e-book requirements www.formatyourebook.com.

Bob Boze – for quietly persisting and helping me get the book into print format. Thanks heaps!

Wanting more?

Additional minute taking resources and articles can be found at:
www.minutesmadness.wordpress.com

Still not enough? Then join the minutes madness:

Facebook:
www.facebook.com/groups/minutesmadness"
www.facebook.com/minutesmad/

LinkedIn:
https://nz.linkedin.com/in/robyn-bennett-5997b0121
https://www.linkedin.com/groups/7062295

The above groups provide additional support, access to resources, a place to ask questions of other members or just download, offload or share a win!

Follow me:
Twitter:
@minutesmad1 #writeminutes #minutetaking
Pinterest:
https://nz.pinterest.com/minutesmadness/

Contact me:
E-mail: minutesmadness@xtra.co.nz

Printed in Great Britain
by Amazon